The Awakened Chronology

books of ~
~ *Mark Willoughby*

A Message To The World

Compiled: The Awakened Chronology
and   A Message to the World ©2021, Mark Willoughby,
Hampton Roads, Va.
Editing services provided by Crickyt J. Meyer
Production services by J. Scott Wilson
ISBN: 978-1-952773-33-4

Preface

The Awakened Chronology and A Message to the World are both some of things I experienced in my life and have observed. It holds within what I witnessed in my dreams and what the spirit of the Lord revealed to me- the understanding He gave unto me. I started to look at life differently just to get an understanding of both inner and outer experiences in life and of the things I witnessed others experiencing. Now I know that there's is a divine infinite spirit that is working on our behalf for the greater good. God as we know him, or YHWH in the Hebrew word, is in control of everything that is happening right now and even from the beginning of Earth's foundation. He existed before time even mattered. Even if we try to wrap our heads a round it, we can't fully understand His ways. His ways exist on a higher plane of consciousness than ours. So, seek to experience life as it is and experience the spiritual unseen world as it is. Do what is needed in the physical life, so the spiritual side can embody it though faith, by the letting the Holy Spirit guide your steps.

Contents

The Awakened Chronology

A Message To The World

The Awakened Chronology

What do you really know about the <u>Bible</u>? For many people, from my perspective, they read it to understand themselves in the word at that present moment in time. But, as 'believers', these words in the Bible are prophecy, and are spirit, yet so often we believers use it occasionally; when needed, for our churches or for help dealing with our family members.

The Bible, as we understand it to be, is a book of facts and of truth; also, about instructions we need to follow and learn. It contains why we need to obey the words of God and His precepts and how to understand God's words. The Bible is from the generations unto the next generations and on forevermore: If you know thy truth then the truth shall set you free. Then the most high will wake up HIS people spiritually and individually, one-by-one, from every nation. The world will keep looking for a sign and will not see any except prophesy fulfilled, nonetheless for He, God, has blinded the eyes of Israel because they hardened their hearts in the wilderness and didn't listen to or take heed of the prophet Isaiah. John 12:40 KJV "He hath blinded their eyes, and hardened their heart; that they should not see with their eyes, nor understand with their heart, and be converted, and I should heal them."

2 Timothy 2:15 (KJV) said: "Study to shew thyself approved unto God, a workman that needth not to be ashamed, rightly dividing the word of truth.

Therefore, study and read God's words for yourself, to know yourself in God, so you can know how you are and where you stand with Him, by the leading of the holy spirit, *Ruach Hakodesh* in Hebrew, in your life, in order to be an example of Christ, as His disciples did. The Hebrew word *Talmid*, or discipline, suggests learning as a student of the body of Christ who must present his or herself as a living sacrifice, being holy and set-apart as his Children. The Hebrew word *Qodeshim* which means set-apart from the world- as true believers in the Messiah would be.

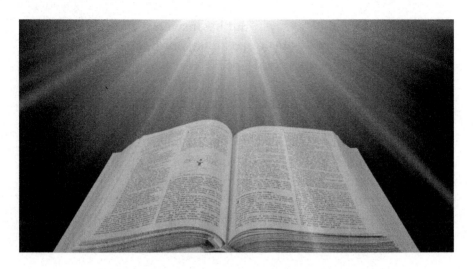

Chapter One: The Awakening Truth

In the beginning, we all know that God created the heavens and the earth and God rested on the seventh day. But what about His *words*, His words that give wisdom and understanding to inspired the prophets and guidance to Jesus' disciples- before biblical scholars could call it the Bible, before prophets and disciples wrote the 66 books divided into Old and New Testaments, before the devil in the spiritual realm tempted Jesus while in the wilderness of the desert, even before the spirit of God moved over the waters when the earth was in darkness and in chaos or when He separated the waters from the waters to create the firmament up above?

Matthew 4:4 (KJV) says, "But he answered and said, "It is written, Man shall not live by bread alone, but by every word that proceedeth out of the mouth of God."

Luke 11:28 (NLT) states "Jesus replied, "But even more blessed are all who hear the word of God and put it into practice." But to the people that said 'Crucify him', trying to stop the Messiah's goodness, the works of God out of the mouth of Christ, attempting to stop His disciples from preaching "the good news" unto others about God the Father and His goodness, - to *those* people the words of their own religious scrolls were from the mouth of God.

In the beginning, the word was with God and the word is still with God. John 1:1 (KJV) "In the beginning was the Word, and the Word was with God, and the Word was God." God's words could not be troubled to them that believe in Him and follow His words. Even before the concept of time as man knows it- the passing of a day into night, God existed and birthed light as a cycle. Psalm 33:6 (NIV) "By the word of the Lord the heavens were made, their starry host by the breath of his mouth." Yahweh's words are what breaks the darkness, even before the earth could be fully formed. Genesis 1:3 (KJV) "And God said let there be light: and there was light."

Scientific evidence cannot prove God's mystery of the world and prove humanity's existence, simultaneously. The Bible that we know today is a Devine destiny to reach believers in this current time, from our forefather's or from our ancestral descendants. In the 6th century B.C according to Wikipedia; The first couple books that were written by the prophet Moses; the Pentateuch, common to the Torah, The Qur'an, and the Old Testament, were Genesis, Exodus, Leviticus, Numbers, and Deuteronomy. Yet the Book of Enoch wasn't included in modern Bibles, along with many other books like those of the Apocrypha – which means hidden – and includes Maccabees one and two, the Wisdom of Solomon and others. What of the Book of Jasher or the Gospel of Thomas?

Genesis 5:24 (KJV) clearly states, "And Enoch walked with God: and he was not; for God took him." These first five books and others form the 39 included in the modern Old Testament and are paired with the 27 books of the New Testament, written centuries later by mankind: according to Biblical and Bible scholars.

Even before Adam and Eve were on Earth and Eve was deceived in the garden of Eden into eating the forbidden fruit from the tree of knowledge of good and evil, the words of the Most High were still in the heavenly places. The Hebrew word *Leechol* means eat or to eat, to take in mind consuming words of conversation. Hosea 10:13 (NIV) "But you have planted wickedness, you have reaped evil, you have eaten the fruit of deception, because you have depended on your own strength and many warriors." Psalms 19:1 (NIV) "The heavens declare the glory of God; the skies proclaim the work of his hands." There even seem to be different levels of Heaven. In 2 Corinthians 12: 2 (NKJV) the Apostle Paul said, "I know a man in Christ who fourteen years ago- whether in the body I do not know, or whether out of the body I do not know, God knows— such a one was caught up to the third heaven."

Lucifer, who once was the bright and morning star and a beautiful singer, perfect in all of his ways to God, was struck out of heaven with one third of the angels that he had deceived. Because of his disobedient rebelliousness, he was expelled out of Heaven. He was cast out into the second heaven (outer space) and down to Earth. Lucifer and his demons travel, roaming around the Earth and in people lives at the same time. Luke 22:3 (NIV) "Then Satan entered Judas, called Iscariot, one of the Twelve." And Judas went the chief priests and the officers of the temple guard and discussed with them how he might betray Jesus. They were delighted and agreed to give him money. He consented and watched for an opportunity to hand Jesus over to them.

Job 1:6-12 (NIV) "One day the angels came to present themselves before the Lord, and Satan also came with them. The Lord said to Satan, 'Where have you came from?'

Satan answered the Lord, 'From roaming throughout the earth, going back and forth on it.'

Then the Lord said to Satan, 'Have you considered my Servant Job? There is no one on Earth like him; he is blameless and upright, a man who fears God and shuns evil.'

'Does Job fear God for nothing?' Satan replied. 'Have you not put a hedge around him and his household and everything he has? You have blessed the work of his hands, so that his flocks and herds are spread throughout the land. But now stretch out your hand and strike everything he has, and he will surely curse you to your face.'

The Lord said to Satan, 'Very well, then everything he has is in your power, but on the man himself do not lay a finger.'

Then Satan went out of the presence of the Lord."

We learn from Job's tale, the Devil has no power of his own, nor have his demons. Therefore, he's limited to what he can do to believers – unless we hand it over to him, despite all the chaos that's happening to people and around our lives has believers. Fear not who can kill the body, but fear who can destroy and cast both body and soul into eternal damnation. There is only one true powerful God force, which is God the Creator. All power and authority is within Him and around Him, for He Himself is powerful; all praise belongs to Him.

2 Peter 2: 4 (KJV) "For if God spared not the angels that sinned, but cast them down to hell, and delivered them into chains of darkness, to be reserved for judgment."

Isaiah 14:12 (KJV) "How art thou fallen from heaven, O Lucifer, son of the morning! How art thou cut down to the ground, which didst weaken the nations!"

Jude: 14-15 (KJV) "And Enoch also, the seventh from Adam, prophesied of these, saying, Behold, the Lord cometh with ten thousands of his saints, to execute judgment upon all, and to convince all that are ungodly among them of all their ungodly deeds which they have ungodly committed, and of all their hard speeches which ungodly sinners have spoken against him."
And Lucifer wanted to be like God.

Isaiah 14:13-14 (KJV) "For you hast said in thine heart, I will ascend into heaven, I will exalt my throne above the stars of God: I will sit also upon the mount of the congregation, in the sides of the north: I will ascend above the heights of the clouds, I will be like the Most High."

It was the devil's intent from the beginning to stop the Creator's plans for His children. Through the hurt and pain of the early prophets and disciples, both before and after Christ, it was God's desire to make them believe in themselves, to have spiritual strength, to bring forth the things He'd invested in them throughout dreams, visions and experiences. In all their traveling to different places, such as in Africa, they were to create a well written, well-read doctrine in one formal format – the Old and New Testament that scholars refer to as The Bible – while, according to the British Library, the Ethiopian bible is recorded as having eighty-eight books which is the largest biblical canon. Indeed the Most High has a plan for all His true believers; a divine intervention for them to receive His words through faith, and by faith reading and hearing the word of the Almighty and putting it to practice. By taking heed of these texts, through through Christ, followers will be taught by God's word. We are indeed saved as believers through Him, the Christ, through faith and by grace.

But, as believers, we are no more under the six hundred and thirteen laws of Moses, but under the grace of God. Matthew 5:17-18 (WEB) "Don't think that I came to destroy the law or the prophets. I didn't come to destroy, but to fulfill. For most certainly, I tell you, until heaven and earth pass away, not even one smallest letter or one tiny pen stroke shall in any way pass away from the law, until all things are accomplished."

For God has put the commandments and the laws on the table of people's hearts and has made a covenant with men. Jeremiah 31:33 KJV states, "But this shall be the covenant that I will make with the house of Israel; After those days, saith the Lord, I will put my law in their inward parts, and write it in their hearts; and will be their God, and they shall be my people." The book of Romans 13:8 (KJV) states, "Owe no man any thing, but to love one another: for he that loveth another hath fulfilled the law." Deuteronomy 6, verses 6-9 instructed "And these words, which I command thee this day, shall be in thine heart: And thou shalt teach them diligently unto thy children, and shalt talk of them when thou sittest in thine house, and when thou walkest by the way, and when thou liest down, and when thou risest up. And thou shalt bind them for a sign upon thine hand, and they shall be as frontlets between thine eyes. And thou shalt write them upon the posts of thy house, and on thy gates."

For many years, Christian theologians, archaeologists, and Biblical scholars tried to unravel the dead sea scrolls and other ancient artifacts, piecing them together. Even the Egyptologists tried to understand the ancient Egyptian writing and hieroglyphs on ancient Egyptian scrolls and the Pyramids and how it was created, to see if events in the Bible ever occurred. For instance, the Ark in the days of Noah and Moses delivering the chosen people, the Israelites, out of Egypt from bondage in the book of Exodus. Amos 9:7. KJV "Are ye not as children of the Ethiopians unto me, O children of Israel? saith the LORD. Have not I brought up Israel out of the land of Egypt? and the Philistines from Caphtor, and the Syrians from Kir?"

Many, such as Atheists, believe the Bible to be fictitious stories or myths, while BioLogos believe that the Bible is non-fiction, containing events which have occurred in fact.

It is true the Bible has numerous translations in various languages in order to serve as a manual or guide, give us insight spiritually, and suggest how to live in these last days. The Bible provides believers with wisdom, knowledge, and understanding. These words of experiences passed down from the prophets to the late forefathers and unto the current disciples; have been rewritten again and again in many different languages. By the 20th century, several versions of the Bible exist. For example, King James Version, New King James Version, New Living Translation, English Standard Version, New International Version, and the Blue Letter Bible. Other digital versions uploaded on the internet can be downloaded to your smart devices as audiobooks so you can listen to the word of the Most High and what Yahweh is saying to His people.

The words of the Most High are true. Therefore, it is Jesus (or Yeh-shu-ah in Hebrew) that keeps our path straight. Since the world is full of evil, we are more likely to do what we want or feel like doing and God had given us free will to do so. Yet, with the Bible and the comfort of the Holy Spirit, which Jesus has given us as a gift, indeed we have the power to listen to the spirit of God or to the devil that works against followers of Christ. The Holy Spirit is in each of us to guide us to the truth with internal conviction. At the same time, it's up to us to choose how we want to live our life on God's earth, whether to read His words and reconcile with Him or not.

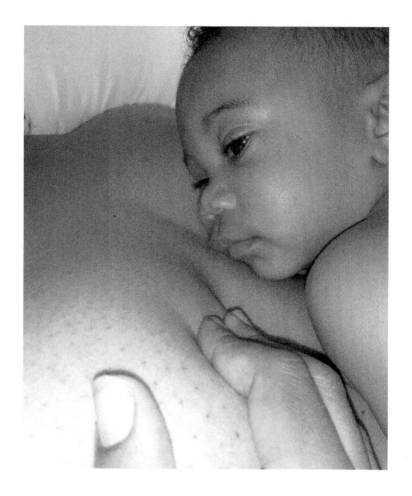

Chapter Two: The God That Is Within You

The Bible said that God knew us before we were formed in our mother's womb. Jeremiah 1:5 (KJV) "Before I formed thee in the belly, I knew thee; and before thou camest forth out of the womb I sanctified thee, and I ordained thee a prophet unto the nations." God taught us into existence; you were planted as seed of faith, spirituality, to do something great on earth for a specific time and for a specific reason. The God that is within you as a believer is way greater than you can imagine. As a believer, you have greatness deep down inside of you.

1 John 4: 4 (KJV) says, "Ye are of God, little children, and have overcome them: because greater is he that is in you, than he that is in the world." For He spoke your name out of heaven with a purpose.

John 8:12 ESV says, "Again Jesus spoke to them, saying, "I am the light of the world. Whoever follows me will not walk in darkness, but will have the light of life."

Because of God's grace, as believers we are now saved through faith by the Messiah. It is Christ that birthed his purpose for us through Yahweh over two thousand years ago, for He makes the way clear for believers, to make way for the Holy Spirit. As in Hebrew the Ruach Ha Kodesh means to set apart, we move up into our lives has believers. Therefore, you have a God given purpose to fulfill at a certain time, just like the Messiah. God the Father is still with all believers.

As for the Devil, he doesn't care if you go to church as believer and hear the word of God, as long as you don't use it in the way you should-- to change your life and that of others. The dark forces of this world can deceive you from your purpose, which the Lord (Adonai in Hebrew) has put on you as His faithful. This world as we know it as Christians is like a quicksand, ready to quake your spirit, to take you off your journey as a true believer in Christ. As Christians, we have a purpose to fulfill. God wants what you have in you to push out into the world; whether you are gifted to write, sing, make music, perform poetry, dance, act, teach, or speak his word – to be a positive vessel of encouragement, to make people steadfast and stand firm in the world. Whatever you're gifted with, use it in this life before the Almighty, unto the grace of God. Don't hold back on the blessing that the Holy Spirit has revealed unto you; the time is now, even as you are reading this.

The Lord will open the chronology of your life, and why you were born in the first place, in that significant time and place. Why you happen to be in the situation that you're in now. He gives you the power of faith to overcome the pain and the hurt in your life. You could have become a stillborn in your mother's womb, but God himself in His infinite grace and mercy kept you. So, you have a purpose in this life. Unfortunately, many don't achieve their divine purpose and take the other side of the road. Their seed didn't fall on good grounds, so they digressed spiritually and instead fed their ego.

Matthew 13:3-9 (KJV) "And he spake many things unto them in parables, saying, Behold, a sower went forth sow; and when he sowed, some seeds fell by the way side, and the fowls came and devoured them up: some fell upon stony places where they had not much earth: and forthwith they sprung up, because they had no deepness of earth. And when the sun was up, they were scorched, because they had no root, they withered away. And some fell among thorns; and the thorns sprung up and choked them: But other fell into good ground, and brought forth fruit, some an hundredfold, some sixtyfold, some thirtyfold. Who hath ears to hear let him hear."

The only ability that the Devil has in this life is to make believers into targets. Not because of who we are as true believes; but because of what we possess within as a believer in Christ. But God has made your hands like a rod of iron to do His works, things that you couldn't imagine you can do. It is the spirit of God that resides within you that makes you stronger. In times when I'm weak as a person in Christ, I've learned to lean on Him when I'm shaken. God makes me steadfast, for He planted my feet on solid ground, holding me steady with His words which are burning deeply in my soul. I learned how to fix my eyes on His words, so my path can be straightened. Thus as a firm and true believer, I choose to keep my eyes on the prize. Psalms 34: 4 said KJV. "I sought the Lord, and he heard me, and delivered me from all my fears."

In life as believers we go through things that we cannot understand and fear that what we cannot see with our own two eyes; but don't be afraid, everything starts in the spirit. Fear weakens the spirit of God that is within believers and can make us feel vulnerable or lose sight of who we are has a believer in Christ. In life, you probably have been confused; perhaps not known where you stand or lacked a sense of identity. Realize that life is always a series of turning points, knocking you off track. Just remember, you are still on the potter's will- safe and secure. Plus, you got the Holy Spirit for direction, reminding you of who you really are in Christ has a truth believer. Our adversary, the Devil, is up against you, but we as believers are more than conquerors. Through Him that delivers us from the evil ones, we know ourselves in God.

The Devil is the master of deception. 1 Peter 5:8 (KJV) "Be sober, be vigilant; because your adversary the devil, as a roaring lion, walketh about, seeking whom he may devour. So be careful. You are on this earth to be tested and tried, so don't lose your faith has a true believer or sense of who you are. You are on a God given journey, and if you don't know exactly what it is yet, listen to the sprite of guidance. That spirit will guide you has a believer to what your purpose is, if you simply let His spirit lead you. The Holy Spirit will then reveal all truth to you. You are called to be awakened from your drunkenness and from your slumber so be wise and be vigilant. So be mindful of who you around, and who around you. watch your surroundings. Remember the word of God. Matthew 10:16 (KJV) "Behold I send you forth as sheep in the midst of wolves: be ye therefore wise as serpents, and harmless as doves."

Chapter Three: When All Else Fails, Trust God

God, the lifeline to my spirit, the center of my faith for my salvation, whom I richly believe in, is a God that cannot change. He is the vines to my soul and the tree to my life, for He will not let me wither nor shrivel or fade away. He is the solid rock to my inner man; I know I can rest-assured in His arms. His words make me into a wise man. I will praise Him and give Him thanks; for I am His and He is mine. God is a very present help in the time of trouble; when I call, he's there. When, I pray, he draws near. I will keep Him my

God, for He is the author of my faith. In Him, I'm fearful and wonderfully crafted by His hands into His likeness. He is my God, and I am His child; He made me to throw spears of strong words of faith by day and to make the weak strong in times like these, to kill the vampires of the soul by night. God maketh a shield unto my right hand, and the helmet of salvation unto my head. His breast plate of righteousness is fashioned unto my chest and His sword is fitted into my right hand. Yes, I will always rest in His loving arms. I will glorify His name, for His words purify my habitat and keep me from snares, set out to devour me in time of weakness. Jehovah, my provider, will feather me from their traps that devils set out for me amongst snakes and wolves.

When I was in the wilderness, they encamped me with fears but didn't harm me. He protected me. They attacked, but their weapons didn't touch me, for He chased them away. Any words from them caused stumbles and choked them from deep within, for their words couldn't hurt me. He, my God, shielded me. Their will was to chastise me, like in the days of Jeremiah. They got their fair share, but He protected me in the days of my youth and has held me in His unchanging hands since. When my mind is clouded, I can hear Him speak to me, for His confident voice resides in my soul in the darkest times. Therefore, I will always meditate on His scriptures and contemplate day and night on His grace. He always brightens my mind and keeps me in oneness with His spirit, reassuring me in Him. I am His and He is mine. He is the lighthouse to my path and is the light that shines from within it. I will abide in Him and He in me, for He is my God. I will construct a house of worship deep within His temple of my soul. When I am weak, God words will encourage me, and my enemies will not see me falter. This too, whatever the negativity, will pass. Good words will always build me up in difficult times and will keep my face high.

INNER
CONFLICT

Chapter Four: Fights - If You Are Distracted, You Are Defeated.

His Faith in me is deeper and the fight is stronger than the adversaries I encounter. The patience of life made me stronger, despite my inner anger. It's He that rescued me from my negative thoughts of life. It's He who purged my spirit and opened my soul to the Holy Ghost. It's He who healed me and kept my fruits ripe when

Willoughby

my soul was barren, when I wasn't fit for the journey. It's He who said "I will make your feet strong to make steps like soldiers on the battle field." However, the biggest fight we face in our life, is the fight with our inner self and that clash deep within. If we aren't careful, that same enemy that we fight deeply within can also affect others, even if it escapes our notice. Not even knowing that we are doing it to ourselves, we can hurt our family members, friends, spouse, and even co- workers.

I call it the quiet, secret enemies. For Jeremiah 17:9 (KJV) states "The heart is deceitful above all things, and desperately wicked: who can know it?" (Note that these troubles target the mind, but Father God speaks to the hearts.) The amounts of my enemies irritate my spirit in times of danger. I will fear them not or quash the spirit of God. If I say, "God is not in me" and squelch the Holy Spirit because of fears, then I'm giving my power that my heavenly Father has given to me to my enemies. Then I'm doubting my God for what is rightfully mine and God-given. He hates to see His children shaken without holding firm to His faith; with that I never fold. So, I learned to be still and know. For now, I can sleep in peace at night and still feel the presence of the Lord around me. He scattered my enemies away and keeps me safe. I may struggle with others and fight those that fight against me, but ultimately the Lord keeps me out of their circles of evil and of wickedness. For the wicked fight evil with evil amongst themselves; then He, the Most High God, will stumble the wicked unto the wicked with blindness and with one breath slay them amongst themselves; but in all peace the Most High One will cover the innocent ones from all sorts of evil if they take heed of their surroundings. In a room full of temptations, He will always prepare a window of escape. But every man is to his own conviction; even when he is convicted by the Spirit, or by His spirit. James 1:14-15 (NIV) "But each person is tempted when they are dragged away by their own evil desire an enticed. Then, after desire has conceived, it gives birth to sin; and sin, when it is full-grown, gives birth to death."

The words of my enemy's mouth, incarcerate my spirit and pierce my soul, putting my feet in shackles from speaking upright and true. However, the Most High, Elohim, God the Father understands my tears when my soul and heart cries out in prayers. In God, I will be confident and in myself, for He kept me this far from them, kept me safe. I learn from those who spitefully hurt me and stand with those who spiritually uplift me. When I am hurt, I can see the actions of aggressors set to rain like dark clouds that hover over me. In their season, my God will shelter me from their sound, which burns my soul like hot coals. My God has always healed my wounds from their negative energy trying to corrupt my spirit. His blessings made ways and sheltered me from such stormy seasons, even when enemies kept rushing in like a tsunami from the ocean. My God will keep my feet planted like brick paving the streets against the groan of a ship anchored to the asphalt. I will not gravitate or levitate to the surface of waters, neither will adversaries see me drowning or pleading for help. Calm as a dove it the midst of chaos, even when everything goes under. As the slander from their tongue revolts against me, I will always anchor myself in Him and the Lord will always keep me in a positive state of mind.

The saying is truth that when men come upon a deep sleep you open the ears of men; Therefore you came to me in a dream in the form of a cloud, the very wrath of a thunderstorm for you were displeased with me and my stiffnecked ways. When you saw me upon that old ship that was anchored you had mercy upon me for you steared my soul to the seashore. For that I give you thanks, for sparing my life, for paving the way for us and aligning our future in the way it should be. I will always praise you, O Lord, even when I'm weak in spirit and when I'm strong. Your blessings multiply in me, everything starts from deep within. I give you thanks, O Lord for the way you had created me in my situation. For it is my situation that has defined me. Therefore, my choices bring life or death from my mouth when I speak. Oh Lord, please put good words in my mouth, words of prosperity and longevity. You are the God who reigns over all people's lives, but it is you that brings peace my life.

Nevertheless it's Yeshua Ha'Mashich in Hebrew, The Messiah, that suffered greatest for our sins. It was His blood that was shed for us on Calvary, Jesus Christ, in English. His name, Christ, derives from the Greek word 'Iesous' from Latin 'Ieses' to the Greek word, 'Christos' – to be like Christ. The Anointed one, Yeshua Ha'Mashiach, died for our sins.

Chapter Five: Evil

Jeremiah 29:11 (KJV) "For I know the thoughts that I think toward you, saith the Lord, thoughts of peace, and not evil, to give you an expected end."

He is the light house to lighten our souls as His true believers in life, for YHWH is great in all of His ways.

Matthew 10:33-39 (ESV) "But whoever denies me before men, I also will deny before my Father who is in heaven. Do not think that I have come to bring peace to earth; I have not come to bring peace, but a sword. For I have come to set a man against his father, and a daughter against her mother and a daughter-in-law against her mother-in-law. And a person's enemies will be those of his own household. Whoever loves father or mother more than me is not worth of me, and whoever loves son or daughter more than me is not worthy of me. And whoever does not take his cross and follow me is not worthy of me. Whoever finds his life will lose it, and whoever loses his life for my sake will find it."

Proverbs 28:1-3 (NIV) "The wicked flee though no one pursues but the righteous are bold as a lion. When a country is rebellious, it has many rulers, but with a ruler of discernment and knowledge, maintains order. A ruler who oppresses the poor is like a driving rain that leaves no crops."

No wonder God separated the light from the darkness, paralleling circumstances that people face in life, and said that the light was good, in the book of Genesis. We are still the apple of His eyes, precious ones, not the Angels in heaven, but we as His true believers; or an individual believer, need to walk in His light and stay in the narrow lane. Some people cling to the darker side of life, following the masses; to the point where no love is found in them. Proverbs 24: 1-2 (NKJV) clearly states, "Do not be envious of evil men, nor desire to be with them, for their heart devises violence, and their lips talk of troublemaking."

Those evil men never cease to oppress the poor, for the darkness of one's heart shows no fear, love, wisdom, knowledge, or respect to God's ways, nor unto His people's. Spirits of darkness overshadow and overcast their minds and hearts, showing no love or humility to one's brother or sister in life. Ephesians 2:3-3 (KJV) Among whom also we all had our conversation in times past in the lusts of our flesh, fulfilling the desires of the of flesh and of the mind; and were by nature the children of wrath, even as others." The savage lifestyle becomes their philosophy in life, breaking both men's Laws and God's Laws, therefore all men's laws are unlawful, but the laws of the Most High are not; furthermore respect their laws and give them no reason to judge one's self.

Proverbs 28 4:8 (NIV) "Those who forsake instruction praise the wicked but those who heed it resist them. Evildoers do not understand what is right, but those who seek the Lord understand it fully. Better the poor man whose walk is blameless than the rich whose ways are perverse. A discerning son heeds instruction, but a companion of gluttons disgraces his father. Whoever increases wealth by taking interest or profit from the poor amasses it for another, who will be kind to the poor." For they have no conviction in heart, always fight to oppress the poor. We tend to be spiritual people thinking to ourselves that we've got limitless grace in God through Christ; and rarely ask if we should continue living comfortable in sinful nature. Romans 6:1-2 (KJV) "What shall we say then? Shall we continue in sin, that grace may abound? God forbid. How shall we, that are dead to sin, live any longer therein?"

On the other side, the wicked are turning their hearts to sexual immorality, raping, killing and all kinds of malicious acts to one another. From what they see, hear, and feel, it starts altering their emotions from the images in their mind and the indignation of their ways, leaving no rationale to thoughts of perspective or life itself on a greater scale. These evil spirits or dark entity forces are always moving over our world's troposphere. In demonstrating fact, around our countries and in our daily lives, they are always ready to ignite one's mind in a split second to cause great clashing with each other, causing fights and inner turmoil in one's life, causing great chronic depression and anxiety that can lead to suicide. These spirits of inner distraction are not to be taken lightly. The damage goes from generations to generations, like a never-ending chain. Examining world and the life you're living is very mind- blowing and can be difficult to understand.

Chapter Six: Spirits

Inside every human being there is a spirit man that God has set around our soul, the spirit of good. Others may open themself to the spirit of evil, but the Holy Spirit is a free gift to anyone that want to receive His spirit. The spirit of God is for anyone who seeks him diligently.

Paul said in Ephesians 6:12 (KJV) "For we wrestle against not flesh and blood, but against principalities, against powers, against the rulers of the darkness of this world, against spiritual wickedness in high places." These evil spirits we believers face in our life and even inside ourselves on a day to day basis are far more than what psychology and psychiatrists can touch upon. As believers we can identify it in others but sometimes, we cannot identify it within ourselves. That is why when one is driven to commit suicide, or to take another person life, we cannot identify where it stems from. In other words, people will try to treat the presence of evil spirits by finding ways to kill them by drinking, smoking, or living as a recluse or a reckless, ridiculous lifestyle to find inner peace. Both good and evil are in our human nature. It all comes down to one thing- the choices we make.

Matthew 12:29 (KJV) "Or else how can one enter into a strong man's house, and spoil his goods, except he first bind the strong man? And then he will spoil his house."

These evil spirits come from self-worthiness, self-pity, jealousy, lust, and by showing signs of malicious behavior to one another. They are also present when man attempts to get praise and power from certain authorities. However, evil spirits can show up in an otherwise good-willed person unbeknownst to them, bringing severe anger to their soul. Life is a gift filled with blessings and lessons at the same time. That is why believers need to walk in the spirit of God, to withstand the lust of the flesh, and to manage our emotions.

Life is surrounded with both negative and positive energies from people and things. Energies attract energies and like attracts like. For instance, our three main senses that draw us to these evil and perverse spirits are sight, hearing, and touch by which evil seeks to get a chance to encounter our feelings. In other words, evil spirits disperse around our lives and can cause an effect from one person to another's life. This, although God has given us five senses to discover, use to navigate through life and to sense right from wrong. Like attracts like and energy attracts energy by the things we watch and do, creating an impact on our lives based on the types of people that we are around. Life can make you both determined and deterred at the same time from your future and your eternity, influenced by the way you live. We as believers can be determined to have a fully affirmed faith in God The Creator while acknowledging that evil spirits move throughout our world, corner to corner throughout the earth.

2 Timothy 1:7 (KJV) "For God hath not given us the spirit of fear; but of power, and of love, and of a sound mind."

Hosea 4:6 (NKJV) "My people are destroyed for lack of knowledge. Because you have rejected knowledge, I also will reject you from being priest for Me; Because you have forgotten the law of your God, I also will forget your children."

In other words, God has given his children as true believers a Spirit of Self-Control. As spiritual beings and as human beings, for Father God has given His believers the Spirit of Faith and not of fear, love and not of lust, like and not of hate, truth and not of deception. There is no generational blindness to this evil; but a spiritual awareness and awakening to test everything that you see and/or hear, before you do, and to have an understanding before you choose, to choose right by having a knowledge in all your doings. Beware of skepticism, of doubting the Holy Spirit. Indeed, have a cognitive mind to reality and learn how to withstand the pitfall of the adversary. The Spirit of Lord is always out to comfort us as believers by leading us to all truth, by way of the Holy Spirit. Therefore, trust God, and walk not in the flesh but in the spirit, so you may succumb to temptation and lust for the flesh.

Galatians 5:16 (KJV) "This I say then, Walk in the Spirit, and ye shall not fulfil the lust of the flesh."

Be still and know that the core of the soul, your spirit, is at the center of your mind, intangible to the devil's reach and tamper. We as believers unknowingly can be deceived, by those evil spirits which can navigate through our mind, affecting our mind, will, and emotion. Such entities can create dry places that cause great disturbance to one's life or even spiritually open the door other evil, even serving to inject legions of troublesome spirits into oneself, if not careful. In doing so, they spread forth the Devil's plan to entice a believer to do his will or try to deceive other people. If that person is spiritually blinded by the devil's devices, or to the spiritual world in general, if he or she cannot identify the real intent, or to surmise the outcome of that manipulated path, he or she can be deceived. To combat this, always walk the path of God the Father, regardless of circumstances presented.

Proverbs 4:23 (KJV) "Keep thy heart with all diligence, for out of it are the issues of life." Above it all, guard your heart, and let life itself distinguish a person's behavior from any wickedness of that person's heart. The hearts of men are wicked and their intentions thereof, by the mouth of that person, will flow like the rivers of waters. In Hebrew, it meant Mayam, which is 'life' and his or her words will follow, blazing like fire.

Proverbs 15:1 (KJV) "A soft answer turneth away wrath, but grievous words stir up anger." Take heed to these words, for you will be tested; and when it is so, you are being tempted.

1 Peter 3:9 (NIV) "Do not repay evil with evil or insult with insult. On the contrary, repay evil with blessing, because to this you were called so that you may inherit a blessing."

Therefore, believers should beware of sharp edges, extremity, cruel words from thyself and others. Always be sober minded, not judgmental, but stray away from all criticism. At the same time, embrace it, acknowledging a different person's ways and path in their doings. Be steadfast in your own doings and let the truth guide you as a believer when dealing with people, bearing in mind they are still in life process themselves. Romans 14:13 (KJV) "Let us not therefore judge one another any more: but judge this rather, than no man put a stumbling-block or an occasion to fall in his brother's way." So, judge not others, but put to task good judgment, discernment, considering your own actions.

Matthew 10:16 (ESV) "Behold, I am sending you out as sheep in the midst of wolves, so be wise as serpents and innocent as doves." The fear of the Lord is the knowledge of wisdom for nothing is wasted. You are fearfully and wonderfully made by the mighty hands of God, as the works of God, and perfect in your own way, even in your imperfection. Your heavenly Father is perfect in all of His ways.

Do unto others as you would have them do unto you

Chapter Seven: Together We are One Through God in Christ

Galatians 3:24-29 (KJV) "Wherefore the law was our schoolmaster to bring us unto Christ, that we might be justified by faith. But after that faith is come, we are no longer under a schoolmaster. For ye are all the children of God by faith in Christ Jesus. For as many of you as have been baptized into Christ, have put on Christ. There is neither Jew nor Greek, there is neither bond nor free, there is neither male or female: for ye are one all one in Christ Jesus. And if ye be Christ's, then are ye Abraham's seed, and heirs according to the promise."

Romans 11:1, I Say then, has God cast away his people? Certainly not! for I also am an Israelite, of the seed of Abraham, of the tribe of Benjamin.

For this I have seen. In the middle of 2018, behold for the Lord as shown me a mystery in a dream. In a marvelous, expensive skyscraper tower above the mist of the clouds in the depths of the clear blue sky, I was looking throughout the window while standing about 500 ft away from the window. Where I was, it was quiet for the most part. Soon, I saw a shape of a cloud in the form of my country, Jamaica, and then a large patch of cloud in the shape of America, slowly moving and attracting itself to the other. I quickly moved closer to the window to get a longer, closer look. I only got a little bit of a glimpse of the clouds from my dream. After a couple of seconds, I got another glimpse as the clouds shifted away, past my peripheral vision. It was then then I heard the voice of the Lord.

Deep in my spirit, He said unto me "Write the book." I was getting distracted by the imagery in my dream shortly after that and I woke. What I understood from this dream is that the Father wants me to join these two compartmented books together as one. For we must chose how we want to live our life, that path is forged by our choices. Nevertheless Judah and Benjamin come together in formation, but slowly.

Together we are one nation of people according to the Father's plans. Unto Him as believers we must show gratitude in Him and unto others, as the Messiah did when he was teaching the Israelites and his disciples back in his own time, to love one another as you love yourself. Likewise, do as God has loved us, with an everlasting love.

However, that day will come when the Lord's people will flee to the hills of Judea. Psalms 69:35-36 (NIV) "For God will save Zion and rebuild the cities of Judah. Then people will settle there and possess it; the children of servants will inherit it, and those who love his name will dwell there."

Romans 10:12-13 (KJV) "For there is no difference between the Jew and the Greek: for the same Lord over all is rich unto all that call upon him. For whosoever shall call upon the name of the Lord shall be saved.

John 1:-11-14 (KJV) "He came unto his own, and his own received him not. But as many as received him, to them gave he power to become the sons of God, even to them that believe on his name: Which were born, not of blood, nor of the will of the flesh, nor of the will of man, but of God. And the Word was made flesh, and dwelt among us, (and we beheld his glory, the glory as of the only begotten of the Father,) full of grace and truth."

For His love is a divine intervention to our lives, to save us from damnation, even in our selfish ways. Those who have lost loved ones and are still anticipating reunion, I pray that you keep your heart pure even in the difficult times that we are facing now. I pray that you will meet them again. Nothing is new under the sun, as time is showing us in the dreadful nations, we are living in but know that everything works for good. Those who love the Lord thy God, let not your mind be worried or troubled. Set your hearts and your mind on Him, even in the rough times. Together we believers are one with God. Therefore, always keep your faith rising above the failures of this life, which create great fears for you.

Ephesians 5: 6 NLT "Don't be fooled by those who try to excuse these sins, for the anger of God will fall on all who disobey him." You have seen the outcome of others; so always remember, stick with Him. He knows what is best for a believer, so stick with Him! Don't put all of your values into temporarily meaningless things that you see or on this Earth but keep your treasures within you. Set your mind and talents on heavenly things, for such is the kingdom of heaven. Place your value on heavenly things, for there will be treasures for you there also. Seek the kingdom of God that is within thyself, for there you will find peace.

Matthew 13:44-55 (KJV) states, "For the kingdom of heaven is like unto treasure hidden in a field; which when a man hath found, he hideth, and for joy thereof goeth and selleth all that he hath found, and buyeth that field. Again, the kingdom of heaven is like unto a merchant man, seeking goodly pearls: Who, when he had found one pearl of great price, went and sold all he had and bought it. Again, the kingdom of heaven is unto a net, that was cast into the sea, and gathered of every kind: Which, when it was full, they drew to shore, and sat down, and gathered the good into vessels, but cast the bad away. So shall it be at the end of the world: angels shall come forth, and sever the wicked from among the just, and shall cast them into the furnace of fire: there shall be wailing and gnashing of teeth.

Jesus saidth unto them, Have ye understood all these things? They say unto him, Yea, Lord. Then said he unto them, Therefore every scribe which is instructed unto the kingdom of heaven is like unto a man that is a householder, which bringeth forth out of his treasures things new and old. And it came to pass, that when Jesus had finished these parables, he departed thence. And when he was come into his own country, he taught them in their synagogue, insomuch that they were astonished, and said, Whence hath this man this wisdom, and these mighty works? Is not this the carpenter's son? Is not his mother called Mary? And his brethren James, and Joses, and Simon, and Judas?"

Exodus 19:5 (NKJV) states, "Now therefore, if you will indeed obey My voice and keep My covenant, then you shall be a special treasure to Me above all people; for all the earth *is* Mine." For the Gentiles are one through Jesus Christ the Messiah that has grafted the body of Jews. The Lord will welcome thy heart of reconciliation back with him through faith in Jesus name just as Peter did to Cornelius who was an Italian. Acts 10:34-43 (KJV) "Then Peter opened his mouth, and said, of a truth I perceive that God is no respecter of persons: But in every nation he that feareth him, and worketh righteousness, is accepted with him. The word which God sent unto the children of Israel, preaching peace by Jesus Christ: (he is Lord of all). That word, I say, ye know which was published through all Judaea, and began from Galilee, after the baptism which John preached; How God anointed Jesus of Nazareth with the Holy

Ghost and with power; who went about doing good, and healing all that were oppressed of the devil; for God was with him. And we are witnesses of all things which he did both in the land of the Jews, and in Jerusalem; whom they slew and hanged on a tree: Him God raised up the third day, and shewed him openly; Not to all the people, but unto witnesses chosen before God, even to us, who did eat and drink with him after he rose from the dead. And he commanded us to preach unto the people, and to testify that it is he which was ordained of God to be the Judge of quick and dead. To him give all the prophets witness, that through his name whosoever believeth in him shall receive remission of sins." We as believers save not by works but by faith in Jesus' name, through grace. But for the formation of Christianity with the factsthat Constantine formed Christianity was formed under the name Roman Catholicism with other religions to suppress the peoples of the nation. Kinsmen and Kinswomen keep a very close intimate relationship with Christ Jesus, the messiah. He knows they that know Him. As believers we're not saved by denomination, we are saved through faith in God's grace. He that survives to the end will be saved to the end of ages, for the Shepard knows His sheep and the sheep know their Shepard's voice; that is our Father which is in heaven.

Romans 16:17-19 (NIV) "I urge you, brothers and sisters, to watch out for those who cause division and put obstacles in your way that are contrary to the teaching you have learned. Keep away from them. For such people are not serving our Lord Christ, but their own appetites. By smooth talk and flattery, they deceive the minds of naïve people. Everyone has heard about your obedience, so I rejoice because of you; but I want you to be wise about what is good, and innocent about what is evil."

Revelation 2:9 (KJV) said, "I know thy works, and tribulation, and poverty, (but thou art rich) and I know the blasphemy of them which say they are Jews, and are not, but are the synagogue of Satan."

We as believers of all nations are His lost sheep and He is the keeper of them all, for He's always out to find and protect them. Therefore, as we look up to the heavens in all directions, we will be influenced by our emotions, our sensibility. Don't lose hope in the Lord that you serve but rejoice in all gladness and there you'll find satisfaction in Him and not the world. Do the things that please Him so He can be pleased with you. In addition, enjoy life while waiting patiently and with great humility.

Matthew 7:6 (KJV) Christ said, "Give not that which is holy unto the dogs, neither cast ye your pearls before swine, lest they trample them under their feet, and turn again and rend you."

Beware of passive-aggressive behaviors in people but let kindnesses and long-suffering speak for itself. Above all, keep your composure, with self-control. Though emotional control is the key to life itself, withdraw from yourself, from inner anger, and replace that with love. There you will find happiness and peace despite all the negativity that is around. Pray in the Spirit by having a positive, passionate personality, with good energy toward yourself and others. Watch, and study their motives. Be righteous and do good unto others, for 'such is life'.

Matthew 25:31-46 (KJV) "When the Son of man shall come in his glory, and all the holy angels with him, then shall he sit upon the throne of his glory: And before him shall be gathered all nations: and he shall separate them one from another, as a shepherd divideth his sheep from the goats: And he shall set the sheep on his right hand, but the goats on the left. Then shall the King say unto them on his right hand, Come, ye blessed of my Father, inherit the kingdom prepared for you from the foundation of the world: For I was an hungred, and ye gave me meat: I was thirsty, and ye gave me drink: I was a stranger, and ye took me in: Naked, and ye clothed me: I was sick, and ye visited me: I was in prison, and ye came unto me. Then shall the righteous answer him, saying, Lord, when saw we thee an hungred, and fed thee? or thirsty, and gave thee drink? When saw we thee a stranger, and took thee in? or naked, and clothed thee? Or when saw we thee sick, or in prison, and came unto thee? And the King shall answer and say unto them, Verily I say unto you,

Inasmuch as ye have done it unto one of the least of these my brethren, ye have done it unto me. Then shall he say also unto them on the left hand, Depart from me, ye cursed, into everlasting fire, prepared for the devil and his angels: For I was an hungred, and ye gave me no meat: I was thirsty, and ye gave me no drink: I was a stranger, and ye took me not in: naked, and ye clothed me not: sick, and in prison, and ye visited me not. Then shall they also answer him, saying, Lord, when saw we thee an hungred, or athirst, or a stranger, or naked, or sick, or in prison, and did not minister unto thee? Then shall he answer them, saying, Verily I say unto you, Inasmuch as ye did it not to one of the least of these, ye did it not to me. And these shall go away into everlasting punishment: but the righteous into life eternal."

John 10:1-18 (KJV) says, "Verily, verily, I say unto you, He that entereth not by the door into the sheepfold, but climbeth up some other way, the same is a thief and a robber. But he that en-tereth in by the door is the shepherd of the sheep. To him the porter openeth; and the sheep hear his voice: and he calleth his own sheep by name, and leadeth them out.
And when he putteth forth his own sheep, he goeth before them, and the sheep follow him: for they know his voice. And a stranger will they not follow, but will flee from him: for they know not the voice of strangers. This parable spake Jesus unto them: but they un-

derstood not what things they were which he spake unto them. Then said Jesus unto them again, Verily, verily, I say unto you, I am the door of the sheep. All that ever came before me are thieves and robbers: but the sheep did not hear them. I am the door: by me if any man enter in, he shall be saved, and shall go in and out, and find pasture. The thief cometh not, but for to steal, and to kill, and to destroy: I am come that they might have life, and that they might have it more abundantly. I am the good shepherd: the good shepherd giveth his life for the sheep. But he that is a hireling, and not the shepherd, whose own the sheep are not, seeth the wolf coming, and leaveth the sheep, and fleeth: and the wolf catcheth them, and scattereth the sheep. The hireling fleeth, because he is a hireling, and careth not for the sheep. I am the good shepherd, and know my sheep, and am known of mine. As the Father knoweth me, even so know I the Father: and I lay down my life for the sheep. And other sheep I have, which are not of this fold: them also I must bring, and they shall hear my voice; and there shall be one fold, and one shepherd. Therefore, doth my Father love me, because I lay down my life, that I might take it again. No man taketh it from me, but I lay it down of myself. I have power to lay it down, and I have power to take it again. This commandment have I received of my Father."

Revelation 2:10 (KJV) says, "Fear none of those things which thou shalt suffer; behold, the devil shall cast some of you into prison, that ye may be tried; and ye shall have tribulation ten days: be thou faithful unto death and I will give thee a crown of life."

Joel 2:32 (KJV) clearly states, "And it shall come to past, that whosoever shall call on the name of the Lord shall be delivered: for in mount Zion and in Jerusalem shall be deliverance, as the Lord hath said, and in the remnant whom the Lord shall call."

Turn your eyes to the teaching and the writing of the prophet Malachi, which was and still is the word of God, for He sees the good and evil deeds on the earth of the people. To the good ones, don't fill yourself with fears from within yourself or dread yourself to the ground, but fear the Lord thy God with love and respect. Cleanse yourself from all unrighteousness and apprehension of nervousness and of shakiness. Be firm in your faith, for He the Lord is with you until the end of the age.

James 1: 25-27 (KJV) "But whoso looketh into the perfect law of liberty, and continueth therein, he being not a forgetful hearer, but a doer of the work, this man shall be blessed in his deed. If any man among you seem to be religious, and bridleth not his tongue, but deceiveth his own heart, this man's religion is vain. Pure religion and undefiled before God and the Father is this, To visit the fatherless and widows in their affliction, and to keep himself unspotted from the world.

Hebrews 13:5 (NIV) "Keep your lives free from the love of money and be content with what you have, because God has Said, 'Never will I leave you, never will I forsake you.'"

A Message To The World:

What I Have Seen in Dreams

Chapter One: The Vision

Joel 2:28 (KJV) "And it shall come to pass, afterward, that I will pour out my spirit upon all flesh;
and your sons and your daughters shall prophesy, your old man shall dream dreams, and your young man shall see visions"

There is a time, place and season for everything. The spirit of the Lord came upon me, one Sunday afternoon. He said, "Share your dreams and vision unto the people in the world." He that have an ear, let him hear what the word of the Lord says.

My first dreams from the Lord started In Jamaica when I was just a teenager. In the dream, I stood in my front yard outside of my gate and heard the spirit of the Lord speak to me, saying, "Look over there and tell me what you see." I felt his presence on the left side of me, even though I couldn't turn to see his face, but I could feel the presence of God all over me. I looked up and my vision caught the image of New York City. I gazed out at the Atlantic Ocean and started to question, as a strange feeling came upon me. I asked in my mind, "Lord, how am I going to get over there when you know I can't swim that far." Looking out at the ocean, it was clear even in the dream the water meant something to me.

He read my thoughts and confidently said, "Don't give it any thought, I'll get you there. You will go through a season of hard times, of testing, but I'll be there to strengthen you through the bad weather."

I woke up from my dream, which was my first direct contact

with the Lord.

My second dream occurred when I was twenty one, again, standing in my front yard at the same place! To the right of me, I saw the stop sign that was on the other side of the sidewalk and then, the arm of the Lord. He punched His fist into the ground and His arm went right back up. It was like the hand of a fiery giant!

My third dream happened when I was living in Portsmouth, Virginia in 2012. I can remember it was a dark and a gloomy night. Myself and two other people were walking on the sidewalk, when the spirit of the Lord came upon me, showing a message written in clouds, *'Get yourself ready before 2015!'* The words slowly faded, like heavy thick smoke. I looked to my right and saw the moon red as blood. This caused a very terrifying feeling to come over me. Although I didn't know what the dream meant, but I believed one day I would.

Around 2013, I have a fourth dream. Feeling very hungry and tired on my way home from work, I went into a restaurant to order something to eat. That same terrifying feeling came upon me with a warning, *'Tell everyone this is going to happen very soon.'* Before I could say anything, the sky burst open with a loud noise. People were running for their lives. It was pitch black. All over the city people were getting into their cars trying to drive to safety. But, there was nowhere to hide.

Chapter Two: Breaking Silence

Everything I have seen since I was a teenager and till now, it's from the Lord. With research, I've found that all my dreams line up with the Bible Scriptures. He that have an ear, let him hear what the word of the Lord says.

Ezekiel 8:17-18 (KJV) "Then he said unto me, hast thou seen this, O son of man? Is it a light thing to the house of Judah that they commit the abominations which they commit here?
For they have filled the land with violence and have returned to provoke me to anger: and, lo, they put the branch to their nose. Therefore will I also deal in fury: mine eye shall not spare, neither will I have pity: and though they cry in mine ears with a loud voice, yet will I not hear them."

I am only a messenger of the Lord. He that has an ear, let him hear the words the Lord said to me. The Lord has led me to these three books of the Bible: Joel, Ezekiel, and Amos. He that have an ear, let him hear what the word of the Lord says.

Joel 1:14-15 (KJV) "Sanctify ye a fast, call a solemn assembly, gather the elders and all the inhabitants of the land into the house of the Lord your God, and cry unto the Lord. Alas for the day! For the day of the Lord is at hand and as destruction from the almighty shall it come."

1 Thessalonians: 5-3 (KJV) "For when they shall say, Peace and safety; then sudden destruction cometh upon them, as travail upon a woman with child; and they shall not escape."

My fifth dream, again, was very gloomy. While walking very slowly through a business company, something strange came upon me. At first, I heard people yelling at the top of their lungs, saying, "Take me! Please take me." I looked down on the ground and saw money scattered everywhere. Looking up, I saw different spiritual portals, like small tunnels in the ceiling of the building. People had been reported missing and others were running for their lives. One guy I saw running knocked into my shoulder, yelling at a taxi driver. I heard him say, "Please! Take me to California. I have a briefcase full of money in my right hand. Please take me, anywhere, I don't care".

But the taxi man said to him "Your money is no good to me now." Then he put his car in reverse and then pulled off at full speed.

He that have an ear, let him hear what the word of the Lord says. The days of the Lord's wrath seem very terrible.

Ezekiel 7:18-19 (KJV) says, "They shall also gird themselves with sack cloth, and horror shall cover them; and shame shall be upon all faces, and baldness upon all heads. They shall cast their silver in the streets and their gold shall be removed: their silver and their gold shall not be able to deliver them in the day of the wrath of the Lord. They shall not satisfy their souls neither fill their bowels: because it is the stumbling block of their iniquity."

He that have an ear, let him hear what the word of the Lord says. The Lord spoke to me, "Because they are a rebellious nation. Just like in the days of Moses, I will bring destruction."

My sixth dream from the Lord was a still, dark night. I was running with my little cousin, holding her hand. I made a right at a gate that was halfway open. Taking my first steps inside the premises, I see an empty land with grass everywhere. A man called out from the road, "Hey you! come here." He drove near to the sidewalk. I turned and looked at him. Again, he declared, "Come Here!" I ignored his voice and walked off into the outer field. There I saw a medium size shiny ball glowing which slowly moved towards me. I was overcome by a sensation of humility. The light sparkled so beautifully, continuously glowing as it moved toward to me. It was as bright as the moon in the sky. A loud noise suddenly erupted from the sky, scaring me half to death!

Turning my head, gazing up, I witnessed a massive pillow of dark reddish cloud, moving fast before me, like a volcano eruption. And there was the Devil himself, hovering at the forefront of the ominous cloud, as tall as two stacked domestic ladders. He had a mean, ugly face, with twisted horns protruding from his head. His eyes were red and black swirled together like the pits of Hell. In his left hand, he held a spear and his whole body was crimson as he roared from the cloud like a lion, scowling down and straight into my eyes, with his mouth wide open.

Listen to me! The devil is here to kill, steal, and destroy every individual causing them to deceive themself into his own troupe and he can even show up as an Angel of light! Don't be deceived, we are in the last days. The Devil himself is gathering up his army.

2 Corinthians 11: 14 (NASB) "No wonder, for even Satan disguises himself as an angle of light."

My seventh dream, was punctuated by screaming and moaning. I witnessed people looking very devastated, yelling to the sky. Everywhere I looked, people were killing other people. Human blood was everywhere- all over cars and running from puddles on the street. Men were killing each other, even chopping other's heads off and holding it up in their hands.

I didn't understand that dream. I was very scared and terrified with nowhere to run, surrounded by noise all around me. Covering my ears, I knelt on the ground. Then, people started shouting, "No more killing! Please, no more killing!" Everywhere I turned, people were dying left and right. Lifting my head, I looked to the right and saw the moon turned to the color of blood. The sun was nowhere to be found in the sky. The world covered with darkness and blood everywhere. People had fallen in the streets, bodies on top of bodies. The dead kept piling up as far as I could see.

Joel 2:30-31 (KJV) Says, "I will shew wonders in the heavens and in the earth, blood and fire and pillars of smoke. The sun shall be turned into darkness and the moon into blood before the great and the terrible day of the Lord come."

He that have an ear, let him hear what the word of the Lord say's. The Lord told me to tell you, that when the moon turns to blood this is signifying death. Death is at hand.

In Amos 1:3-11 (KJV) it states "Thus saith the LORD; For three transgressions of Damascus, and for four, I will not turn away the punishment thereof; because they have threshed Gilead with thresh-ing instruments of iron: But I will send a fire into the house of Haz-ael, which shall devour the palaces of Benhadad. I will break also the bar of Damascus, and cut off the inhabitant from the plain of Aven, and him that holdeth the sceptre from the house of Eden: and the people of Syria shall go into captivity unto Kir, saith the LORD. Thus saith the LORD;

For three transgressions of Gaza, and for four, I will not turn away the punishment thereof; because they carried away captive the whole captivity, to deliver them up to Edom: But I will send a fire on the wall of Gaza, which shall devour the palaces thereof: And I will cut off the inhabitant from Ashdod, and him that holdeth the sceptre from Ashkelon, and I will turn mine hand against Ekron: and the remnant of the Philistines shall perish, saith the Lord GOD. Thus saith the LORD; For three transgressions of Tyrus, and for four, I will not turn away the punishment thereof; because they delivered up the whole captivity to Edom, and remembered not the brotherly covenant: But I will send a fire on the wall of Tyrus, which shall de-vour the palaces thereof. Thus saith the LORD; For three transgres-sions of Edom, and for four, I will not turn away the punishment thereof; because he did pursue his brother with the sword, and did cast off all pity, and his anger did tear perpetually, and he kept his wrath forever"

Therefore, let us be steadfast and unremovable of the sight of these actions that were and still are taking place, see fit that it causes no effect.

Chapter Three: The Leading of the Holy Spirit

My last dream was in August 2014. The Lord is sending a message to the world. Our God is a God of order. In the natural eye, it's like nothing is happening. Spiritually, everything is coming to an end. *Psalm 37:-23-24 (NLT) "The Lord direct the steps of the godly, He delights in every detail of their lives, Though they stumble, they will never fall, for the Lord holds them by the hand."*

I thought to myself, this is it, and started to question myself, whether there was a point to my dreams, something I should be doing. On May 6th, 2016, in the middle of the night, I woke from a disturbing, unreasonable dream that the Lord came for his people. The sting of death was in my heart and, to my knowledge, I was on the verge of destruction. Amongst all different kinds of people, I felt I was in a deserted place. Minding my own business, without a shock of a doubt, I felt something hit me deep inside my heart. I wondered to myself why I felt like this, why I was in this predicament. Pleading with God to forbid such embarrassment, before I could repent for my sin, the hour had cometh on everyone around me. I was ashamed and terrified.

He was revealing another vision, about our life foretold, our eternity. Before I could think twice, I saw people's sins played out before them like flat screen television. Wherever they went it followed. If they hid, it hid with them. If they turned, it turned. If they ran, it moved with them. There was no escape from their own sins.

The atmosphere was insidious. Everyone was witnessing their own sins, with unhealthy lifestyles and all manner of evil, past hurtful words, even some with senseless killing.

I felt armed and proudly repentant. No man is perfect or proven to be, but we will be tried and tried in the time of our flesh. Trying to remember it clearly as possible, after waking took me to *Revelation 3:10-11 (NIV) "Since you have kept my command to endure patiently, I will also keep you from the house of trial that is going to come on the whole world to test the inhabitants of the earth. I am coming soon. Hold on to what you have, so that no one will take your crown."*

In May of 2016. I sensed the spirit of the Lord move upon me again in the middle of the night. Clearly, He wanted me to relive something. The day before, my co-worker invited me to her father's church. I when with her to the second service. The church is called Freedom Fellowship, which is in Virginia Beach, Virginia. I observed as the church followed through with praise and worship. One song stood out to me by the name of *Set a Fire Down in My Soul*. The congregation worshiped and praised the Lord. I was amazed as they sang the chorus over and over and over again as people were getting delivered.

Pastor Rick, who is the lead Pastor, preached about 'The Big Picture', which was a very enthusiastic topic. Then he shifted his sermon to a different motive, one which strategically opened my eyes about when the Lord returns and how we should be prepared. Everything I viewed in my dreams; he was giving a small hint about it. The deeper he went with his words, the deeper I felt the Lord speaking to my heart, about bringing forth my dreams and vision. The more he talked the more I could envision people getting delivered.

Acts 2:1-4 says, "And when the day of Pentecost was fully come, they were all with one accord in one place. And suddenly there came a sound from heaven as of a rushing mighty wind, and it filled all the house where they were sitting. And there appeared unto them cloven tongues like as of fire, and it sat upon each of them. And they were all filled with the Holy Ghost, and began to speak with other tongues, as the Spirit gave them utterance."

Acts 2:15-21 says, "For these are not drunken, as ye suppose, seeing it is but the third hour of the day. But this is that which was spoken by the prophet Joel; And it shall come to pass in the last days, saith God, I will pour out of my Spirit upon all flesh: and your sons and your daughters shall prophesy, and your young men shall see visions, and your old men shall dream dreams: And on my servants and on my handmaidens I will pour out in those days of my Spirit; and they shall prophesy: And I will shew wonders in heaven above, and signs in the earth beneath; blood, and fire, and vapor of smoke: The sun shall be turned into darkness, and the moon into blood, before the great and notable day of the Lord come: And it shall come to pass, that whosoever shall call on the name of the Lord shall be saved."

He preached on preserving the Holy Spirit and on the coming of Jesus Christ, on what going to happen to us. Right then, I started having an encounter with the Holy Spirit, reflecting on my dreams.

After the service, alter call was requested for anyone that need to receive the Holy Spirit. In about 20 minutes, the entire church made their way the alter! The majority were getting delivered, while others where crying for the peace of God on their life. I met Pastor Rich and felt a connection right away. I revealed to him what the Lord as laid upon my heart. He told me to bring it on my next visit. I prayed and followed the Lord's instruction and did so. I was led by the Lord to share my dreams, and I pray that this may be good to anyone that reads it. While it is for me to share, it is to serve everyone living.

It has been made clear to me that God is calling young men and young woman to come to Him, especially our young black men. He is earnestly calling that they turn away from evil deeds. Why have the urgency to kill your brothers? You are blinded by the world and worldly things. Why be the victim? Why shed your brother's blood, causing another mother to cry? Why thirst for someone else's life, when you know that the devil doesn't play fair? Turn from evil planning and profanity and repent from your ways. Stop killing. I plead for you to listen to your parents that God put before you as guides. The one you kill will be judge and the one to shed your blood will be judged. Likewise, the one that thirsts for your blood also will be judged. The Bible says after death is the judgement. That judgement is permanent. Turn away from this evil of the world and turn to God.

Chapter Four: Reveal

Proverbs 1:7-22 (KJV) "The fear of the LORD is the beginning of knowledge: but fools despise wisdom and instruction. My son, hear the instruction of thy father, and forsake not the law of thy mother: For they shall be an ornament of grace unto thy head, and chains about thy neck.

My son, if sinners entice thee, consent thou not.

If they say, Come with us, let us lay wait for blood, let us lurk privily for the innocent without cause.

Let us swallow them up alive as the grave; and whole, as those that go down into the pit.

We shall find all precious substance, we shall fill our houses with spoil: Cast in thy lot among us; let us all have one purse: My son, walk not thou in the way with them; refrain thy foot from their path: For their feet run to evil, and make haste to shed blood.

Surely in vain the net is spread in the sight of any bird. And they lay wait for their own blood; they lurk privily for their own lives. So are the ways of every one that is greedy of gain; which taketh away the life of the owners thereof.

Wisdom crieth without; she uttereth her voice in the streets: She crieth in the chief place of concourse, in the openings of the gates: in the city she uttereth her words, saying, How long, ye simple ones, will ye love simplicity? and the scorners delight in their scorning, and fools hate knowledge?

My dreams are so real. Please heed what the Lord is saying.

Trust and obey, trust and obey. That's what I was and am still doing. I did lose sight of God at one point and ignored the voice of Yahweh, finding excuses not to go to church. By slacking off, killing precious time, not focusing on my writing nor praying, I fell victim to myself and feel self-conscious for losing focus, for focusing on my faults and weakness by living in the past. In that state, depression hit me like a whirlwind, which brought me to this day. Once more the lord spoke to me.

On November 6, 2016 the Lord called me, and I can remember it clearly, it was a Sunday night around 6:21 pm. God spoke to my heart and said, "Get in your car and drive to church, I need to have a word with you." I thought about it while sitting on the edge of my bed. I was about to lay down and felt something strange; it was a decision I had to make, a simple decision. Stay in bed or take the opportunity to go to church. I got up, put my shoes on, and drove over to Pastor Rick's church, Freedom Fellowship, which is not too far from where I lived. Arriving at exactly 6:27, taking a look at my smart phone, meant they would be breaking from praise and worship. I'd still have enough time to listen to what God had to say. I entered the church to find it only half full. Taking a seat, I listened to the message about Fear and Faith. Pastor Rick was out for that Sunday night, instead his son was preaching.

What really caught my attention was that he was speaking directly to me. He wasn't looking at me, but I felt it deep in my heart, the word of God piercing through me in ways I can't imagine. The impact was palpable. In the middle of his sermon, the minister said, "What about the book that Lord told you to write? Instead, you at home doing nothing. You have the opportunity to shed some light on the world, but you refuse to do so. I gave you confirmation on top of confirmation and still you doubt my word. Even when I specifically send three people your way, you still doubt me." At that moment, I knew God was speaking directly to me.

I felt like my path was over and sensed a little distress. I felt ashamed because I thought I had let him down. Holding my head down, I reflected on my life, where he took me from and where I am now. They say that when God trying to get to you, he will move mountains just to find you. Whom the Lord loves, He corrects. The power of negativity started falling away and God's peace surrounded me. At the end of the service, there was an alter call and everyone made their way up, including myself.

After service, I waited around while members met and greeted with Pastor Rick's son. Then, I said to him. "I am that person you were talking about." He replied, "That wasn't me. That was the Holy Spirit," and elaborated. "The Lord told me that an author just walked in. I should have of said it over the mic but was caught up doing something and totally forgot all about it. But yeah, He did." The words touched my heart so strongly and a warm spirit came over me. I shed some tears and told him thanks. "Whatever He wants you to do, just do it," my preacher said. "Just write it down. I don't know what it is or what you're writing. What I do know, is that God has a purpose for you. You have a gift and you should use it. You have the gift of writing and God want to use you for His purpose in this life." Then, we prayed.

Chapter Five: Two Roads

Jeremiah 30:2 (KJV) says, "Thus speaketh the Lord God of Israel, saying, Write thee all the words that I have spoken unto thee in a book."

These are not my words but His. I was to relay, to comply what God wants me to do. I thought He was finished with me, but clearly, He wasn't. Please take heed to what I'm writing, guided by Him. He wants me to spread His words to the world and to His people, so it can reach the hearts of the rebellious, cruel, and cynical people in this word.

Why my people, why have you forgotten the words of your God? Still my people are still distracted in this sinful world. Behold, I put out two paths for you to choose, but I can see you're not choosing well. The Devil has got his hands around you, blindfolding with lies, leading you closer and closer to his road. I told you Hell is not for my people, but I can see sin still entices thee.

There are two roads ahead.

Before I choose, you already know which path I'm taking Oh Lord. You knew what is inside my heart before I thought about it. Evidently, I'm blinded by the Devil's devices which captivate my mind mentally. If I choose narrowly, I can dilute from getting distracted, which can bring distress and anguish into my life. Therefore I put my hand in yours so I may walk with you.

So, I choose the road to glory.

(This was on my heart so I decided to put in this this book, for those who need to hear it too.) I put time and effort into this because He wants me to write this down, so the person who need to read this, can read it. As I take a closer look at life, sometimes I wonder. Does fear make us stray away from the Lord's works, even though we usually create our own fear?

2 Timothy 1:7 (KJV) "For God hath not given us the spirit of fear; but of power, and love and of a sound mind."

Job 3:25 (KJV) "For the thing which I greatly feared is come upon me, and that which I was afraid of is come unto me."

1 John 4:1 (KJV) says, "Beloved, believe not every spirit, but try the spirits whether they are of God: because many false prophets are gone out into the world."

So try them and you will know whether they are of God or not. Peace is for those who accept Jesus as their personal Lord and savior, for He has heard your prayers and heard your cries. He will never leave you nor will He forsake you. I put my trust in Him, for He has put a new song in my heart. Lord, I will left His name on high. He commanded His angels to watch over me. He will not let the enemy grab ahold of my feet nor will He make them smite me. He surrounds me with His love and blessings, with His ornament of grace. His mercy follows me.

Jeremiah 29:11 (KJV), "For I know the thoughts that I think toward you, saith the Lord, thoughts of peace, and not of evil, to give you an expected end."

Let His peace take its place in you. Let God be your guidance and refuge. Let Him direct your path to righteousness, for his peace is within you. Have a calm mind and a right spirit; be on fire for the Lord. Trust Him and always acknowledge His ways. Follow His teaching for His words are like steppingstones to glory and a light house to your path. Amen.

1 Thessalonians 5:16-22 (KJV) reminds, "Rejoice evermore. Pray without ceasing. In every thing give thanks: For this is the will of God in Christ Jesus concerning you. Quench not the Spirit. Despise not prophesyings. Prove all things: hold fast that which is good. Abstain from all appearance of evil."

For this is God's words from Him to me: It will be senseless to walk in the flesh and not in the spirit. We lust for things that we see and want, and not seek Him. We must seek Him day in and day out. Every drop of a second that the clock ticks, minute by minute, hour by hour, for He is life and we can't live without Him. Let the blood of Jesus saturate through you like dampened cloth and fill you from deep within. Don't be stagnant, like the lake and the swamp that you see, but be like rivers of running, living waters. Be not like the ocean, for it move on its own pace and drifts slowly. Be active in Christ! Do not be like the waves, going back and forth; there is no growth in that. Be steadfast in the Holy Spirit and hold firm to what you've got, but also do His will.

Luke 10:19 (KJV) tells, "Behold I give unto you power to tread on serpents and scorpions, and over all the power of the enemy: and nothing shall by any means hurt you."

James 1:3 (KJV) speaks, "Knowing this, that the trying of your faith worketh patience."

Brethren, I've been sent here into America to do one thing and that is to write what the Lord wants me to write. He led me with these scriptures that coincide with my dreams. The time has come that all men, women and children shall see the greatness of God, for the time is now. Let His word spread to all sinners, atheists, and backsliders and to all believers that believe in Christ our savior, and to all churches. God is going to roll back the sea, so be steadfast. Now is the time to watch and pray. For we are in the days of Revelation, but the Bible is our guide and, as you can see, everything is now being revealed to us. It is now manifesting both good and evil. Keep a clear mind. Be encouraged and know that He is still with us. The time has come to watch and pray.
Thank you for reading.

Author's Message to the Reader

First and foremost, I must say thank you for taking your precious time to open this short chapter size book up and read what the Lord has shown me by life experience and observations of others. This two short part book is about unfolding your spirit eyes to see what it is the Lord wants you to see. With His scriptures and my life experience, I try to explain why our existence is such a blessing to us and others and why our God is so important to us. Also, I seek to warn of tricks enemies and the Devil use to oppose us against each other and even against ourselves, guided by the Lord's word and messages to me.

It is God's will for us to be one with Him by being one with ourselves and others. Through His influence, I try in the first book, using passages from the Bible and my own understanding, to convey to the readers the bigger picture of what He's trying to make us understand, what He's saying to us individually. "Together we are one with God." The second portion of this book is about what He has shown me, through dreams and why.

On this journey, I have made a choice to change my life, to do God's will. It wasn't *my* intention to do so, but looking back from where he brought me from and the things I couldn't overcome on my own, I had to give Him freedom and space to do His work within me. He made a change in my life and a shift in the universe when He inspired me to write this book before my time on Earth expired. It was simply my time to put God first.

Colophon

Wider Perspectives Publishing, care of James Wilson, has produced works by the following artists,

Edith Blake
Tanya Cunningham-Jones
    (Scientific Eve)
Terra Leigh
Ray Simmons
Samantha Borders-Shoemaker
Bobby K.
    (The Poor Man's Poet)
J. Scott Wilson (TEECH!)
Charles Wilson
Gloria Darlene Mann
Neil Spirtas
Jason Brown (Drk Mtr)
Jorge Mendez & JT Williams
Sarah Eileen Williams
Stephanie Diana (Noftz)
Jack Cassada
Dezz

Chichi Iwuorie
Ken Sutton
Crickyt J. Expression
Lisa M. Kendrick
Cassandra IsFree
Nich (Nicholis Williams)
Samantha Geovjian Clarke
Natalie Morison-Uzzle
Gus Woodward II
Patsy Bickerstaff

Catherine TL Hodges
Martina Champion
Tony Broadway
Zach Crowe
Mark Willoughby
Kent Knowlton
... and others to come soon.

You should really check them out
WPP has also been entrusted with producing
The Poetry Society of Virginia's annual review for 2020
    (Poetry Virginia: 2020)
The Poet's Domain (since vol. 33, 2019)
and
the Hampton Roads Artistic Collective anthologies
    (757 Perspectives vol.1 through...)

HRAC is the Charitable extension
of WPP, periodically choosing a
worthy Hampton Roads Cause and
donating proceeds of an anthology to it.

Check for the above artists on
FaceBook, the Virginia Poetry
Online channel on YouTube, and
other social media.

Made in the USA
Middletown, DE
11 October 2021